cookies

a fine selection of sweet treats

MURDOCH BOOKS

Contents

Wholesome

An abundance of fruit, nuts and seeds star
in these nourishing delights.

Orange polenta biscuits

MAKES 20–22

125 g (4½ oz/½ cup) unsalted butter, softened
80 g (2¾ oz/⅓ cup) caster (superfine) sugar
1 teaspoon orange flower water
finely grated zest from 1 orange
2 eggs
165 g (5¾ oz/1⅓ cups) plain (all-purpose) flour
80 g (2¾ oz/½ cup) polenta

Preheat the oven to 200°C (400°F/Gas 6). Line two baking trays with baking paper.

Combine the butter, sugar, orange flower water and orange zest in a food processor and process until light and creamy. Add the eggs and process until smooth. Add the flour and polenta and pulse until a sticky dough forms.

Transfer the mixture to a piping bag fitted with a 2 cm (¾ inch) star nozzle. Pipe the mixture onto the prepared baking trays to form 7 cm (2¾ inch) crescents. Bake for 15 minutes, or until lightly golden around the edges. Allow to cool on the trays for a few minutes, then transfer to a wire rack to cool completely.

Orange polenta biscuits will keep, stored in an airtight container, for up to 3 days.

Fig and ginger cookies

MAKES 36

Preheat the oven to 180°C (350°F/Gas 4). Line two baking trays with baking paper.

Cream the butter, sugar and vanilla in a medium-sized bowl using electric beaters until pale and fluffy, then add the egg yolk and beat until just combined.

Transfer the butter mixture to a large bowl, add the figs and ginger, and stir to combine. Sift the flour into the mixture and add the bicarbonate of soda and ground ginger. Stir with a wooden spoon until a soft dough forms.

Shape tablespoons of dough into balls, place on the prepared trays 4 cm (1½ inches) apart and flatten slightly. Bake for 10–12 minutes, or until lightly golden around the edges. Allow to cool on the trays for a few minutes, then transfer to a wire rack to cool completely. Repeat with the remaining dough.

These cookies will keep, stored in an airtight container, for up to 4 days.

160 g (5⅔ oz/⅔ cup) unsalted butter, softened
140 g (5 oz/¾ cup) soft brown sugar
1 teaspoon natural vanilla extract
1 egg yolk
95 g (3¼ oz/½ cup) chopped semi-dried figs
90 g (3¼ oz/½ cup) chopped glacé ginger
210 g (7½ oz/1¾ cups) plain (all-purpose) flour
½ teaspoon bicarbonate of soda (baking soda)
1½ tablespoons ground ginger

Chunky chocolate and muesli cookies

MAKES 36

125 g (4½ oz/½ cup) unsalted butter, softened
230 g (8¼ oz/1 cup) soft brown sugar
1 teaspoon natural vanilla extract
1 egg
125 g (4½ oz/1 cup) plain (all-purpose) flour
60 g (2¼ oz/½ cup) self-raising flour
½ teaspoon bicarbonate of soda (baking soda)
40 g (1½ oz/⅓ cup) unsweetened cocoa powder
45 g (1⅔ oz/½ cup) desiccated coconut
130 g (4⅔ oz/1 cup) natural fruit and nut muesli
250 g (9 oz/1⅔ cups) chopped dark chocolate

Preheat the oven to 180°C (350°F/Gas 4). Line two baking trays with baking paper.

Cream the butter, sugar and vanilla in a medium-sized bowl using electric beaters until pale and fluffy, then add the egg and beat until just combined. In a separate bowl, sift together both flours, the bicarbonate of soda and the cocoa powder. Add to the butter mixture with the coconut, muesli and chocolate. Stir with a wooden spoon until a soft dough forms.

Shape tablespoons of dough into balls, place on the prepared trays 5 cm (2 inches) apart and flatten slightly. Bake for 12 minutes, or until crisp on top and lightly golden. Allow to cool on the trays for a few minutes, then transfer to a wire rack to cool completely. Repeat with the remaining dough.

These cookies will keep, stored in an airtight container, for up to 2 weeks.

Pistachio and cardamom cookies

MAKES 30

250 g (9 oz/1 cup) unsalted butter, softened
85 g (3 oz/⅔ cup) icing (confectioners') sugar
½ teaspoon natural vanilla extract
1 teaspoon finely grated lemon zest
50 g (1¾ oz/⅓ cup) pistachio nuts, chopped
280 g (10 oz/2¼ cups) plain (all-purpose) flour
60 g (2¼ oz/⅓ cup) rice flour
1 teaspoon ground cardamom

Line two baking trays with baking paper. Cream the butter, sugar and vanilla in a medium-sized bowl using electric beaters until pale and fluffy. Transfer to a large bowl, add the lemon zest and the pistachios and stir until combined. Sift the flours together into the butter mixture and add the cardamom, then mix with a knife using a cutting motion to form a soft dough. Cover with plastic wrap and refrigerate for 30 minutes.

Preheat the oven to 160°C (315°F/Gas 2–3). Remove the mixture from the fridge and shape tablespoons of dough into balls, then place on the prepared trays 4 cm (1½ inches) apart. Flatten into 4 cm (1½ inch) rounds and bake for 15 minutes, or until lightly golden underneath. Allow to cool for a few minutes on the trays, then transfer to a wire rack to cool completely. Repeat with the remaining dough.

These cookies will keep, stored in an airtight container, for up to 3 weeks.

Fennel wafers

55 g (2 oz/¼ cup) caster (superfine) sugar
2 tablespoons sesame seeds
2 tablespoons fennel seeds
185 g (6½ oz/1½ cups) plain (all-purpose) flour
60 ml (2 fl oz/¼ cup) olive oil
60 ml (2 fl oz/¼ cup) beer
1 tablespoon anise liqueur

Lightly grease a baking tray and line with baking paper. In a small bowl, combine the sugar, sesame seeds and fennel seeds. In a separate, large bowl, sift the flour and a pinch of salt and make a well in the centre. Add the oil, beer and liqueur and mix with a large metal spoon until the dough comes together.

Transfer the dough onto a lightly floured surface and knead until it is smooth and elastic. Wrap the dough in plastic wrap and refrigerate for 30 minutes.

Preheat the oven to 200°C (400°F/Gas 6). Divide the dough in two and roll out each portion between two sheets of baking paper as thinly as possible. Stamp rounds out of the dough using a 4 cm (1½ inch) round cookie cutter—you should get about 40 rounds.

Sprinkle the dough rounds with the sugar mixture, then gently roll a rolling pin over the top of them so that the seeds adhere to the dough.

Transfer the rounds to the prepared tray and bake for 6–8 minutes, then place the wafers under a hot grill (broiler) for 1–2 minutes to caramelise the sugar, taking care not to burn them. Transfer to a wire rack to cool completely. Repeat with the remaining dough.

These wafers will keep, stored in an airtight container, for up to 2 weeks.

2828

Walnut crisps

MAKES 25

Preheat the oven to 160°C (315°F/Gas 2–3). Line two baking trays with baking paper.

Using electric beaters, beat the egg, egg yolk, sugar and vanilla in a medium-sized bowl until combined. Sift the flour into the egg mixture. Stir with a wooden spoon until smooth, then fold in the walnuts.

Shape rounded teaspoons of dough and place them well apart on the prepared trays. Flatten slightly and bake for 15–17 minutes, or until lightly golden and crisp. Allow to cool on the trays for a few minutes, then transfer to a wire rack to cool completely.

The crisps will keep, stored in an airtight container, for up to 2 weeks.

1 egg
1 egg yolk
115 g (4 oz/½ cup) caster (superfine) sugar
½ teaspoon natural vanilla extract
2 tablespoons plain (all-purpose) flour
155 g (5½ oz/1¼ cups) chopped golden walnuts

Banana spice cookies

MAKES 36

185 g (6½ oz/¾ cup) unsalted butter, softened
230 g (8¼ oz/1 cup) caster (superfine) sugar
1 teaspoon natural vanilla extract
1 egg yolk
150 g (5½ oz/1 cup) dried banana chips, chopped
125 g (4½ oz/1 cup) plain (all-purpose) flour
125 g (4½ oz/1 cup) self-raising flour
2 teaspoons ground mixed spice
45 g (1⅔ oz/½ cup) desiccated coconut
2 tablespoons whole cloves, to garnish

Preheat the oven to 170°C (325°F/Gas 3). Line two baking trays with baking paper.

Cream the butter, sugar and vanilla in a medium-sized bowl using electric beaters until pale and fluffy, then add the egg yolk and beat until just combined. Add the banana and stir to combine. Sift the flours into the butter mixture and add the mixed spice and coconut. Stir with a wooden spoon until a soft dough forms.

Shape tablespoons of dough into balls and place on the prepared trays 4 cm (1½ inches) apart. Flatten the balls slightly, then press a clove into the top of each one. Bake for 12 minutes, or until lightly golden around the edges. Allow to cool on the trays for a few minutes, then transfer to a wire rack to cool completely. Repeat with the remaining dough.

Banana spice cookies will keep, stored in an airtight container, for up to 1 week.

Cranberry and hazelnut refrigerator biscuits

MAKES 50

175 g (6 oz) unsalted butter, softened
125 g (4½ oz/1 cup) icing (confectioners') sugar
2 egg yolks
2 teaspoons lemon juice
185 g (6½ oz/1½ cups) plain (all-purpose) flour
110 g (3¾ oz/1 cup) ground hazelnuts
150 g (5½ oz/1½ cups) sweetened dried cranberries
80 g (2¾ oz/½ cup) poppy seeds

Cream the butter and sugar in a medium-sized bowl using electric beaters until pale and fluffy, then add the egg yolks and lemon juice and beat until just combined. Sift the flour into the butter mixture and add the ground hazelnuts. Stir well with a wooden spoon, then stir in the cranberries. Divide the mixture in half.

Scatter half the poppy seeds over a 30 cm (12 inch) long piece of foil. Place half the mixture on the work surface and form it into a 21 cm (8¼ inch) long sausage shape. Transfer the dough to the foil, rolling the dough in the poppy seeds to coat, then roll tightly in the foil to form a neat cylinder, twisting the ends tight. Repeat with the remaining dough and poppy seeds and another piece of foil. Refrigerate the dough for a minimum of 4 hours.

Preheat the oven to 170°C (325°F/Gas 3) and lightly grease two baking trays.

Remove the foil and cut the dough into 8 mm (⅜ inch) slices. Place the rounds on the prepared trays and bake for 12–15 minutes, or until firm and lightly golden. Cool on the trays for a few minutes, then transfer to a wire rack to cool completely.

These biscuits will keep, stored in an airtight container, for up to 1 week.

23

Macadamia and white chocolate cookies

MAKES 25

210 g (7½ oz/1⅓ cups) macadamia nuts
1 egg
165 g (5¾ oz/¾ cup) soft brown sugar
2 tablespoons sugar
1 teaspoon natural vanilla extract
125 ml (4 fl oz/½ cup) olive oil
60 g (2¼ oz/½ cup) plain (all-purpose) flour
30 g (1 oz/¼ cup) self-raising flour
¼ teaspoon ground cinnamon
30 g (1 oz/½ cup) shredded coconut
130 g (4½ oz/¾ cup) white chocolate chips

Preheat the oven to 180°C (350°F/Gas 4). Place the macadamias on a baking tray and bake for 5 minutes, or until lightly toasted. Cool and roughly chop into small pieces with a large sharp knife.

Using electric beaters, beat the egg and sugars in a medium-sized bowl until light and fluffy, then add the vanilla and oil. Sift the flours into the egg mixture and add the cinnamon, coconut, toasted macadamias and chocolate chips. Mix well with a wooden spoon, then refrigerate for 30 minutes.

Lightly grease two baking trays and line with baking paper. Shape tablespoons of dough into balls and place on the baking trays, pressing the mixture together with your fingertips if crumbly. Bake for 12–15 minutes, or until lightly golden around the edges. Allow to cool on the trays for a few minutes, then transfer to a wire rack to cool completely.

These cookies will keep, stored in an airtight container, for up to 1 week.

VARIATION: Dark chocolate chips can be used instead of white chocolate.

Rosemary and raisin cookies

MAKES 24

Preheat the oven to 180°C (350°F/Gas 4). Line two baking trays with baking paper.

Cream the butter, sugars and vanilla in a small bowl using electric beaters until pale and fluffy, then add the egg and beat until just combined. Transfer the mixture to a large bowl. Sift the flour into the butter mixture and add the baking powder, nutmeg, rosemary and raisins. Stir with a wooden spoon until a soft dough forms.

Shape tablespoons of dough into balls, place on the prepared trays 5 cm (2 inches) apart and flatten slightly to make 4 cm (1½ inch) rounds. Garnish the top of each with a rosemary sprig and bake for 12–13 minutes, or until lightly golden. Allow to cool on the trays for a few minutes, then transfer to a wire rack to cool completely.

These cookies will keep, stored in an airtight container, for up to 5 days.

125 g (4½ oz/½ cup) unsalted butter, softened
115 g (4 oz/½ cup) caster (superfine) sugar
95 g (3¼ oz/½ cup) soft brown sugar
½ teaspoon natural vanilla extract
1 egg
250 g (9 oz/2 cups) plain (all-purpose) flour
1 teaspoon baking powder
½ teaspoon ground nutmeg
1 tablespoon chopped rosemary, plus 24 small sprigs, to garnish
125 g (4½ oz/1 cup) raisins

Peach, cinnamon and almond cookies

MAKES 30

160 g (5⅔ oz/⅔ cup) unsalted butter, softened
230 g (8¼ oz/1 cup) caster (superfine) sugar
½ teaspoon natural vanilla extract
1 egg
90 g (3¼ oz/⅔ cup) dried peaches, finely chopped
210 g (7½ oz/1¾ cups) plain (all-purpose) flour
1 teaspoon baking powder
1 teaspoon ground cinnamon
55 g (2 oz/½ cup) ground almonds
50 g (1¾ oz/⅓ cup) blanched almonds, to garnish

Preheat the oven to 190°C (375°F/Gas 5). Line two baking trays with baking paper.

Cream the butter, sugar and vanilla in a medium-sized bowl using electric beaters until pale and fluffy, then add the egg and beat until just combined. Add the peach and stir to combine. Sift the flour and add to the mixture along with the baking powder, cinnamon and ground almonds. Stir with a wooden spoon until a soft dough forms.

Shape tablespoons of dough into balls and place on the prepared trays 5 cm (2 inches) apart. Place a blanched almond on top of each, gently pressing into the dough, and flatten slightly to make 4 cm (1½ inch) rounds. Bake for 12 minutes, or until lightly golden around the edges. Allow to cool on the trays for a few minutes, then transfer to a wire rack to cool completely. Repeat with the remaining dough.

These cookies will keep, stored in an airtight container, for up to 1 week.

Trail mix and honey cookies

MAKES 20

Preheat the oven to 160°C (315°F/Gas 2–3). Line two baking trays with baking paper.

Combine the lime zest, honey, egg whites and vanilla in a medium-sized bowl and whisk until frothy. In a separate, large bowl, sift the flour and add the papaya, pineapple, almonds, pistachios, pepitas, sesame seeds and coconuts. Make a well in the centre, then add the egg white mixture. Stir with a wooden spoon until a soft dough forms.

Shape tablespoons of the mixture into balls, place on the prepared trays 4 cm (1½ inches) apart and flatten slightly. Bake for 15 minutes, or until they are lightly golden around the edges. Allow to cool on the trays for a few minutes, then transfer to a wire rack to cool completely.

Trail mix and honey cookies are best served on the day they are made.

2 teaspoons finely grated lime zest
90 g (3¼ oz/¼ cup) honey
2 egg whites
½ teaspoon natural vanilla extract
30 g (1 oz/¼ cup) plain (all-purpose) flour
60 g (2¼ oz/⅓ cup) finely sliced glacé papaya
2 tablespoons finely sliced glacé pineapple
25 g (1 oz/¼ cup) flaked almonds
35 g (1¼ oz/¼ cup) pistachio nuts, chopped
1 tablespoon pepitas (pumpkin seeds)
2 teaspoons sesame seeds
40 g (1½ oz/¾ cup) flaked coconut
25 g (1 oz/¼ cup) desiccated coconut

Malted milk and oat cookies

MAKES 26

125 g (4½ oz/1 cup) self-raising flour
100 g (3½ oz/1 cup) rolled (porridge) oats
170 g (6 oz/¾ cup) caster (superfine) sugar
40 g (1½ oz/⅓ cup) malted milk powder
65 g (2¼ oz/¾ cup) desiccated coconut
2 tablespoons honey
150 g (5½ oz) unsalted butter

Preheat the oven to 180°C (350°F/Gas 4). Line two baking trays with baking paper.

Sift the flour in a large bowl and add the oats, sugar, milk powder and the coconut. Mix together and make a well in the centre.

Place the honey, 1 tablespoon hot water and the butter in a small saucepan. Stir over low heat until the butter has melted. Pour the butter mixture into the well in the dry ingredients and stir with a wooden spoon until a soft dough forms.

Shape tablespoons of dough into balls, place well apart on the prepared trays and flatten slightly. Bake for 12–15 minutes, or until golden brown around the edges. Allow to cool on the trays for a few minutes, then transfer to a wire rack to cool completely. Repeat with the remaining dough.

These cookies will keep, stored in an airtight container, for up to 1 week.

Date and sesame cookies

MAKES 30

160 g (5⅔ oz/⅔ cup) unsalted butter, softened
185 g (6½ oz/1 cup) soft brown sugar
1 teaspoon natural vanilla extract
1 egg
2 teaspoons sesame oil
160 g (5⅔ oz/1 cup) chopped dates
250 g (9 oz/2 cups) plain (all-purpose) flour
1 teaspoon baking powder
50 g (1¾ oz/⅓ cup) sesame seeds

Preheat the oven to 180°C (350°F/Gas 4). Line two baking trays with baking paper.

Cream the butter, sugar and vanilla in a medium-sized bowl using electric beaters until pale and fluffy, then add the egg and sesame oil, beating until just combined. Add the dates and stir to combine. Sift in the flour and baking powder and stir with a wooden spoon to form a soft dough.

Place the sesame seeds in a small bowl. Shape tablespoons of the dough into balls and press one side down into the sesame seeds. Place on the prepared trays, sesame side up, 5 cm (2 inches) apart, and then flatten slightly to make 4 cm (1½ inch) rounds. Bake for 12 minutes, or until lightly golden. Allow to cool on the trays for a few minutes, then transfer to a wire rack to cool completely. Repeat with the remaining dough.

These cookies will keep, stored in an airtight container, for up to 5 days.

Fig oaties

MAKES 30

125 g (4½ oz/½ cup) unsalted butter, softened
230 g (8¼ oz/1 cup) caster (superfine) sugar
1 egg
2 tablespoons milk
½ teaspoon ground cinnamon
½ teaspoon bicarbonate of soda (baking soda)
115 g (4 oz/¾ cup) sesame seeds
280 g (10 oz/1½ cups) chopped dried figs
125 g (4½ oz/1¼ cups) rolled (porridge) oats
155 g (5½ oz/1¼ cups) plain (all-purpose) flour
6 dried figs, sliced, to garnish

Preheat the oven to 180°C (350°F/Gas 4). Cream the butter and sugar in a medium-sized bowl using electric beaters until pale and fluffy, then add the egg and milk and beat until smooth. Stir in ½ teaspoon salt, cinnamon and bicarbonate of soda. Add the sesame seeds, figs and oats. Sift the flour and fold into the mixture with a wooden spoon.

Shape tablespoons of the dough into balls and place well apart on two ungreased baking trays. Flatten slightly and top with a slice of fig. Bake for 15–20 minutes, or until lightly golden around the edges. Allow to cool on the trays for a few minutes, then transfer to a wire rack to cool completely.

Fig oaties will keep, stored in an airtight container, for up to 5 days.

Pine nut cookies

MAKES 70

270 g (9½ oz/1¾ cups) blanched whole almonds
345 g (12 oz/1½ cups) caster (superfine) sugar
2 egg whites
¼ teaspoon natural vanilla extract
1 teaspoon clear honey, warmed
465 g (1 lb/3 cups) pine nuts
40 g (1½ oz/⅓ cup) icing (confectioners') sugar,
   to dust

Preheat the oven to 190°C (375°F/Gas 5). Line two baking trays with baking paper.

Combine the almonds in a food processor in 2 batches, with 125 g (4½ oz/½ cup) of the sugar in each batch. Process for 30 seconds, or until finely ground.

Mix together the ground almonds and the remaining sugar in a large bowl.

Combine the egg whites, vanilla and honey in a medium-sized bowl and whisk until frothy. Add the egg mixture to the almonds and sugar and stir well. Set aside for 5 minutes.

Sprinkle the pine nuts into a dish, shape tablespoons of dough into balls and roll them in the pine nuts to coat. Place well apart on the prepared trays and sift the icing sugar over. Bake for 10–12 minutes, or until lightly golden. Allow to cool on the trays for a few minutes, then transfer to a wire rack to cool completely. Repeat with the remaining dough.

These cookies will keep, stored in an airtight container, for up to 5 days.

NOTE: You need to grind your own almonds, as this recipe won't work with ready-bought ground ones.

Spicy apple drops

MAKES 20

2 eggs
60 g (2¼ oz/¼ cup) unsalted butter,
melted and cooled
220 g (7¾ oz/1 cup) raw (demerara) sugar
30 g (1 oz/¼ cup) malted milk powder
280 g (10 oz/2¼ cups) self-raising flour
1 teaspoon ground cinnamon
½ teaspoon ground mixed spice
200 g (7 oz) green apple, peeled, cored and
chopped (about 1½ apples)
140 g (5 oz/3⅓ cups) cornflakes
60 g (2¼ oz/½ cup) chopped pecans
icing (confectioners') sugar, to dust
ground cinnamon, to dust

Preheat the oven to 180°C (350°F/Gas 4). Lightly grease two baking trays and line with baking paper.

Using electric beaters, lightly beat the eggs in a medium-sized bowl. Stir in the melted butter, add the sugar and then beat until smooth. Sift the malted milk powder, flour, ¼ teaspoon salt, cinnamon and the mixed spice into the mixture and beat well. Stir in the apple, cornflakes and pecans and mix well.

Shape tablespoons of the dough into balls and place well apart on the prepared trays. Bake for 15–20 minutes, or until lightly golden. Allow to cool on the trays for a few minutes, then transfer to a wire rack to cool completely. When the cookies are cool, dust with the sifted icing sugar and then sprinkle a little cinnamon on top.

These cookies will keep, stored in an airtight container, for up to 5 days.

Almond fruit bread

MAKES 30–40 SLICES

Preheat the oven to 180°C (350°F/Gas 4). Lightly grease a 25 x 8 cm (10 x 3¼ inch) loaf (bar) tin and line it with baking paper.

Whisk the egg whites in a bowl until soft peaks form, then gradually add the sugar, whisking continuously. Continue whisking until very stiff peaks form, and then fold through the flour. Gently fold in the almonds and the glacé fruits. Transfer the mixture to the prepared tin, smooth the surface and bake for 30–40 minutes, or until firm to the touch.

Cool in the tin for 10 minutes, then turn out and peel off the baking paper. Cool completely on a wire rack, then wrap in foil and set aside for 1–2 days.

Preheat the oven to 140°C (275°F/Gas 1) and line a baking tray with baking paper. Using a very sharp knife, cut the loaf into wafer-thin slices. Spread onto the baking tray and bake for 45–50 minutes, until dry and crisp. Allow to cool on the trays for a few minutes, then transfer to a wire rack to cool completely.

Almond fruit bread will keep, stored in an airtight container, for up to 5 days.

3 egg whites
125 g (4½ oz) caster (superfine) sugar
125 g (4½ oz/1 cup) plain (all-purpose) flour, sifted
125 g (4½ oz) whole almonds
100 g (3½ oz/½ cup) glacé cherries
30 g (1 oz) glacé apricots, cut into pieces the same size as the cherries
30 g (1 oz) glacé pineapple, cut into pieces the same size as the almonds

Apricot cookies with lemon icing

MAKES 32

160 g (5⅔ oz/⅔ cup) unsalted butter, softened
170 g (6 oz/¾ cup) caster (superfine) sugar
2 tablespoons marmalade
1 teaspoon natural vanilla extract
200 g (7 oz) dried apricots, chopped
125 g (4½ oz/1 cup) self-raising flour
40 g (1½ oz/⅓ cup) plain (all-purpose) flour
125 g (4½ oz/1 cup) icing (confectioners') sugar
2 teaspoons lemon juice

Line two baking trays with baking paper. Cream the butter and sugar in a medium-sized bowl using electric beaters until light and creamy. Add the marmalade, vanilla and apricots and mix until well combined.

Sift the flours into a large bowl and then stir in the butter mixture. Turn out onto a lightly floured surface and bring together until just smooth. Divide in half. Place each portion on a sheet of baking paper and roll up in the paper to form two logs, 21 cm (8¼ inches) long and 4.5 cm (1¾ inches) thick. Lay on a tray and place in the refrigerator for 15 minutes until firm.

Preheat the oven to 180°C (350°F/Gas 4). Remove the baking paper and, using a serrated knife, cut the logs into 1 cm (½ inch) diagonal slices. Place well apart on the prepared trays. Bake for 10–15 minutes, or until golden. Allow to cool on the trays for at least 5 minutes, then transfer to a wire rack to cool completely. Repeat with the remaining dough.

To make the icing, sift the icing sugar into a small bowl. Add the lemon juice and 3 teaspoons hot water and stir until smooth. Place in a small paper or plastic piping bag. Seal the end and snip off the tip. Decorate the cookies with the icing.

These cookies will keep, stored in an airtight container, for up to 5 days.

Walnut and orange biscotti

MAKES 40

Preheat the oven to 170°C (325°F/Gas 3). Lightly grease a baking tray.

Sift the flour, baking powder and bicarbonate of soda into a large bowl, then stir in the sugar. Combine the eggs, orange zest and vanilla in a bowl and stir with a fork to mix well. Pour the egg mixture into the flour mixture and stir until nearly combined, then, using your hands, knead briefly to form a firm dough. Put the dough on a lightly floured work surface and knead the walnuts into the dough.

Divide the dough into three even-sized pieces. Working with one piece of dough at a time, roll to form a 29 cm (11½ inch) log. Gently pat the surface to flatten the log to a 4 cm (1½ inch) width, then place the three logs on the prepared tray and bake for 30 minutes, or until light golden and firm. Remove from the oven and allow to cool for 15 minutes.

Reduce the oven to 150°C (300°F/Gas 2). When the logs are cool enough to handle, cut them on the diagonal into 1 cm (½ inch) thick slices. Arrange in a single layer on two baking trays and bake for 15 minutes, or until the biscotti are dry, swapping the position of the trays halfway through cooking. Cool on a wire rack.

Biscotti will keep, stored in an airtight container, for up to 3 weeks.

310 g (11 oz/2½ cups) plain (all-purpose) flour, plus extra for rolling
1 teaspoon baking powder
½ teaspoon bicarbonate of soda (baking soda)
170 g (6 oz/¾ cup) caster (superfine) sugar
3 eggs, lightly beaten
finely grated zest from 3 oranges
2 teaspoons natural vanilla extract
250 g (9 oz/2½ cups) walnut halves, lightly toasted and roughly chopped

Pineapple and coconut cookies

MAKES 36

160 g (5⅔ oz/⅔ cup) unsalted butter, softened
230 g (8¼ oz/1 cup) caster (superfine) sugar
1 teaspoon natural vanilla extract
1 egg
2 tablespoons milk
1 teaspoon finely grated lemon zest
95 g (3¼ oz/½ cup) glacé pineapple,
finely sliced
250 g (9 oz/2 cups) plain (all-purpose) flour
1 teaspoon baking powder
45 g (1⅔ oz/½ cup) desiccated coconut
30 g (1 oz/½ cup) shredded coconut, plus extra
to garnish

Preheat the oven to 180°C (350°F/Gas 4). Line two baking trays with baking paper.

Cream the butter, sugar and vanilla in a bowl using electric beaters until pale and fluffy, then add the egg, milk and lemon zest, beating until just combined. Transfer the mixture to a large bowl, add the pineapple and stir to combine. Sift the flour into the mixture and add the baking powder and coconuts, and stir with a wooden spoon until a soft dough forms.

Shape tablespoons of the dough into balls and place on the prepared trays 4 cm (1½ inches) apart. Sprinkle the extra shredded coconut on the cookies and flatten slightly to make 5 cm (2 inch) rounds. Bake for 13 minutes, or until lightly golden around the edges. Cool for a few minutes on the baking trays, then transfer to a wire rack to cool completely. Repeat with the remaining dough.

These cookies will keep, stored in an airtight container, for up to 5 days.

Plain Jane

Simple these may be, but there's nothing ordinary
about these cookie jar essentials.

Jam thumbprints

MAKES 45

250 g (9 oz/1 cup) unsalted butter, softened
140 g (5 oz) icing (confectioners') sugar
1 egg yolk, lightly beaten
90 g (3¼ oz) cream cheese, softened and
cut into chunks
1½ teaspoons natural vanilla extract
1 teaspoon finely grated lemon zest
340 g (11¾ oz/2¾ cups) plain (all-purpose) flour
¼ teaspoon baking powder
½ teaspoon bicarbonate of soda (baking soda)
2 tablespoons each apricot, blueberry and
raspberry jam

Preheat the oven to 180°C (350°F/Gas 4) and grease three baking trays.

Cream the butter, sugar and the egg yolk in a bowl using electric beaters until pale and fluffy, then beat in the cream cheese, vanilla and lemon zest until smooth. Sift the flour, baking powder, bicarbonate of soda and ¼ teaspoon salt into a large bowl and, using a wooden spoon, gradually stir in the butter mixture until a soft dough forms. Set aside for 5–10 minutes, or until the dough firms up.

Shape tablespoons of the dough into balls, place on the prepared trays well apart and flatten slightly to make 4 cm (1½ inch) rounds. Make a small indent in the centre of each and spoon about ¼ teaspoon of apricot jam into one-third of the cookies, ¼ teaspoon blueberry jam into one-third, and ¼ teaspoon of raspberry jam into the remaining one-third of the cookies. Bake for 10–12 minutes, or until lightly golden. Allow to cool on the trays for a few minutes, then transfer to a wire rack to cool completely.

These cookies are best eaten the same day but will keep, stored in an airtight container, for up to 2 days.

Crackle cookies

MAKES 60

Place the chocolate in a heatproof bowl over a saucepan of simmering water, ensuring the bowl doesn't touch the water. Stir until the chocolate is melted. Set aside to cool for 5 minutes.

Cream the butter, sugar and vanilla in a medium-sized bowl using electric beaters until pale and fluffy, then add the eggs, one at a time, beating until just combined. Add the melted chocolate and milk and stir to combine.

Sift the flour, cocoa, baking powder, mixed spice and a pinch of salt into the butter mixture and mix well. Stir the pecans through. Refrigerate for at least 3 hours, or overnight.

Preheat the oven to 180°C (350°F/Gas 4). Lightly grease two baking trays. Roll tablespoons of the mixture into balls and roll each in the icing sugar to coat. Place well apart on the trays. Bake for 20–25 minutes, or until lightly browned. Allow to cool on the trays for a few minutes, then transfer to a wire rack to cool completely. Repeat with the remaining mixture.

These cookies will keep, stored in an airtight container, for up to 2 days.

60 g (2¼ oz) dark chocolate
125 g (4½ oz/½ cup) unsalted butter, softened
370 g (13 oz/2 cups) soft brown sugar
1 teaspoon natural vanilla extract
2 eggs
80 ml (2½ fl oz/⅓ cup) milk
340 g (11¾ oz/2¾ cups) plain (all-purpose) flour
2 tablespoons unsweetened cocoa powder
2 teaspoons baking powder
¼ teaspoon ground mixed spice
85 g (3 oz/⅔ cup) chopped pecans
icing (confectioners') sugar, to coat

Maple brown sugar cookies

MAKES 48

140 g (5 oz) unsalted butter, softened
185 g (6½ oz/1 cup) soft brown sugar
115 g (4 oz/⅓ cup) maple syrup
1 egg yolk
250 g (9 oz/2 cups) plain (all-purpose) flour
½ teaspoon bicarbonate of soda (baking soda)
¼ teaspoon ground cinnamon
¼ teaspoon ground cardamom
125 g (4½ oz/1 cup) icing (confectioners')
sugar, sifted
1½ tablespoons maple syrup, extra
½ teaspoon natural vanilla extract

Preheat the oven to 180°C (350°F/Gas 4). Line two baking trays with baking paper.

Cream the butter and sugar in a medium-sized bowl using electric beaters until pale and fluffy, then add the maple syrup and egg yolk, beating until just combined. Sift in the flour, bicarbonate of soda, cinnamon and cardamom, and stir with a wooden spoon to form a soft dough. Shape the dough into a flat disc, cover with plastic wrap and refrigerate for 20 minutes.

Roll out the dough between two pieces of baking paper to 5 mm (¼ inch) thick. Cut the dough into rings using a 5 cm (2 inch) round cookie cutter, re-rolling the dough scraps and cutting more circles. Place on the prepared trays 4 cm (1½ inches) apart and bake for 8 minutes, or until lightly golden. Allow to cool on the trays for a few minutes, then transfer to a wire rack to cool completely. Repeat with the remaining dough.

To make the maple syrup icing, place the icing sugar, extra maple syrup and vanilla in a medium-sized bowl, and stir to combine. Add enough water to make a smooth, thick, runny consistency. When the cookies are completely cool, drizzle with the maple syrup icing.

These cookies will keep, stored in an airtight container, for up to 3 weeks.

Choc chip cookies

MAKES 16

Preheat the oven to 180°C (350°F/Gas 4). Line a large baking tray with baking paper.

Cream the butter and sugar in a large bowl using electric beaters until pale and fluffy, then add the vanilla and egg, beating until just combined. Add the milk and stir to combine. Sift in the flour and baking powder, stir in the dark chocolate chips and stir with a wooden spoon to form a soft dough.

Shape tablespoons of dough into balls, place on the prepared tray 4 cm (1½ inches) apart and flatten slightly. Bake for 15 minutes, or until lightly golden around the edges. Allow to cool on the tray for a few minutes, then transfer to a wire rack to cool completely.

These cookies will keep, stored in an airtight container, for up to 2 days.

125 g (4½ oz/½ cup) unsalted butter, softened
185 g (6½ oz/1 cup) soft brown sugar
1 teaspoon natural vanilla extract
1 egg, lightly beaten
1 tablespoon milk
210 g (7½ oz/1¾ cups) plain (all-purpose) flour
1 teaspoon baking powder
260 g (9¼ oz/1½ cups) dark chocolate chips

Crumbly cashew cookies

MAKES 36

140 g (5 oz) unsalted butter, softened
145 g (5¼ oz/⅔ cup) caster (superfine) sugar
1 teaspoon natural vanilla extract
1 egg yolk
155 g (5½ oz/1 cup) unsalted cashews, finely chopped
250 g (9 oz/2 cups) plain (all-purpose) flour

Preheat the oven to 170°C (325°F/Gas 3). Line two baking trays with baking paper.

Cream the butter, sugar and vanilla in a medium-sized bowl using electric beaters until pale and fluffy, then add the egg yolk and beat until just combined. Add the cashews and sift in the flour. Stir with a wooden spoon until a soft dough forms.

Shape tablespoons of dough into balls, place on the prepared trays 4 cm (1½ inches) apart and flatten slightly with a fork dipped in flour. Bake for 8–10 minutes, or until lightly golden around the edges. Allow to cool on the trays for a few minutes, then transfer to a wire rack to cool completely. Repeat with the remaining dough.

Crumbly cashew cookies will keep, stored in an airtight container, for up to 2 weeks.

Ginger fingers

MAKES 25

100 g (3½ oz/¾ cup) chopped macadamia nuts
250 g (9 oz/1 cup) unsalted butter, softened
80 g (2¾ oz/⅓ cup) caster (superfine) sugar
100 g (3½ oz) glacé ginger, chopped
250 g (9 oz/2 cups) plain (all-purpose) flour
90 g (3¼ oz/½ cup) rice flour
caster (superfine) sugar, to sprinkle

Preheat the oven to 150°C (300°F/Gas 2). Line a large baking tray with baking paper. Lay the macadamias on another baking tray and toast for 3–5 minutes, or until lightly golden. Set aside to cool.

Cream the butter and sugar in a medium-sized bowl using electric beaters until pale and fluffy. Mix in the ginger and nuts. Sift in the flours and stir with a wooden spoon to form a dough.

Gather the dough into a ball and roll out to a 1 cm (½ inch) thick rectangle. Cut into 3 x 7 cm (1¼ x 2¾ inch) fingers. Place on the prepared tray and sprinkle with the caster sugar. Bake for 35 minutes, or until the ginger fingers are pale golden underneath. Allow to cool on the tray for a few minutes, then transfer to a wire rack to cool completely.

Ginger fingers will keep, stored in an airtight container, for up to 2 days.

Pecan praline cookies

MAKES 24

115 g (4 oz/½ cup) caster (superfine) sugar
125 g (4½ oz/½ cup) unsalted butter, softened
170 g (6 oz/¾ cup) caster (superfine) sugar, extra
1 teaspoon natural vanilla extract
1 egg yolk
250 g (9 oz/2 cups) plain (all-purpose) flour
1 teaspoon baking powder
150 g (5½ oz/1½ cups) whole pecans

Preheat the oven to 160°C (350°F/Gas 2–3). Line two baking trays with baking paper.

To make the praline, combine the caster sugar and 1 tablespoon water in a small saucepan, stirring over low heat until the sugar is dissolved. Use a pastry brush to brush down any excess sugar on the side of the saucepan. Once the sugar is dissolved, stop stirring and continue cooking until the liquid becomes a golden caramel colour. Pour this toffee onto one of the prepared trays, spreading it out evenly. Allow to cool and harden, then break into pieces. Process in a food processor until finely chopped. Re-line the baking tray with baking paper.

Cream the butter, extra sugar and vanilla in a medium-sized bowl using electric beaters until pale and fluffy, then add the egg yolk, beating until just combined. Add the finely chopped praline and stir to combine. Sift in the flour and baking powder and stir with a wooden spoon to form a soft dough.

Shape tablespoons of the dough into small logs and press a pecan into the centre of each. Place on the prepared trays 4 cm (1½ inches) apart and bake for 12–15 minutes, or until lightly golden around the edges. Allow to cool on the trays for a few minutes, then transfer to a wire rack to cool completely.

These cookies will keep, stored in an airtight container, for up to 2 weeks.

Cinnamon circles

MAKES 25

50 g (1¾ oz) unsalted butter, softened
80 g (2¾ oz/⅓ cup) caster (superfine) sugar
½ teaspoon natural vanilla extract
85 g (3 oz/⅔ cup) plain (all-purpose) flour
1 tablespoon milk
2 tablespoons caster (superfine) sugar, extra
½ teaspoon ground cinnamon

Preheat the oven to 180°C (350°F/Gas 4). Line two baking trays with baking paper.

Cream the butter and sugar in a medium-sized bowl using electric beaters until pale and fluffy, then stir in the vanilla. Sift in the flour and add the milk. Stir with a wooden spoon to form a soft dough, gather into a ball and place on a sheet of baking paper.

Press the dough out to a log shape, 25 cm (10 inches) long and 3 cm (1¼ inches) thick. Roll in the paper and twist the ends to seal. Refrigerate for 20 minutes, or until firm.

Cut the log into rounds 1 cm (½ inch) thick. Sift the extra caster sugar and cinnamon onto a plate and roll each cookie in the sugar mixture, coating well. Lay well apart on the prepared trays and bake for 20 minutes, or until lightly golden around the edges. Allow to cool on the trays for a few minutes, then transfer to a wire rack to cool completely.

These cookies will keep, stored in an airtight container, for up to 5 days.

Marble cookies

200 g (7 oz/1⅓ cups) chopped dark chocolate
125 g (4½ oz/½ cup) unsalted butter, softened
230 g (8¼ oz/1 cup) caster (superfine) sugar
1 teaspoon natural vanilla extract
1 egg yolk
2 tablespoons milk
250 g (9 oz/2 cups) plain (all-purpose) flour
½ teaspoon baking powder

Preheat the oven to 180°C (350°F/Gas 4). Line two baking trays with baking paper.

Place the chocolate in a heatproof bowl over a saucepan of simmering water, ensuring the bowl doesn't touch the water. Stir until the chocolate has melted. Set aside to cool for 5 minutes.

Cream the butter, sugar and vanilla in a medium-sized bowl using electric beaters until pale and fluffy, then add the egg yolk and milk, beating until just combined. Sift in the flour and baking powder and stir with a wooden spoon to form a soft dough.

Make a well in the centre of the dough and pour in the chocolate. Using a knife, gently fold through the chocolate to give a rippled effect, being careful not to overmix.

Shape tablespoons of the dough into balls, place on the prepared trays 5 cm (2 inches) apart and flatten slightly. Bake for 12–15 minutes, or until lightly golden around the edges. Allow to cool on the trays for a few minutes, then transfer to a wire rack to cool completely. Repeat with the remaining dough.

These cookies will keep, stored in an airtight container, for up to 1 week.

Anise drops

MAKES 30

Preheat the oven to 180°C (350°F/Gas 4). Line two baking trays with baking paper.

Cream the butter, sugar, vanilla and anise in a medium-sized bowl using electric beaters until pale and fluffy, then add the egg yolk, honey and milk, beating until just combined. Sift in the flours and baking powder and stir with a wooden spoon to form a soft dough.

Shape tablespoons of dough into balls, place on the prepared trays 5 cm (2 inches) apart and flatten slightly. Bake for 10–15 minutes, or until lightly golden around the edges. Allow to cool on the trays for a few minutes, then transfer to a wire rack to cool completely. Repeat with the remaining dough.

These cookies will keep, stored in an airtight container, for up to 5 days.

185 g (6½ oz/¾ cup) unsalted butter, softened
115 g (4 oz/½ cup) caster (superfine) sugar
1 teaspoon natural vanilla extract
1 teaspoon anise extract
1 egg yolk
2 tablespoons honey
1 tablespoon milk
250 g (9 oz/2 cups) plain (all-purpose) flour
90 g (3¼ oz/½ cup) rice flour
1½ teaspoons baking powder
1 teaspoon aniseeds

Classic shortbread

MAKES 16 WEDGES

225 g (8 oz) unsalted butter, softened
115 g (4 oz/½ cup) caster (superfine) sugar,
plus extra for dusting
210 g (7½ oz/1¾ cups) plain (all-purpose) flour
115 g (4 oz/⅔ cup) rice flour

Lightly grease two baking trays. Cream the butter and sugar in a medium-sized bowl using electric beaters until pale and fluffy. Sift in the flours and a pinch of salt and stir with a wooden spoon until it resembles fine breadcrumbs. Transfer to a lightly floured work surface and knead gently to form a soft dough. Cover with plastic wrap and refrigerate for 30 minutes.

Preheat the oven to 190°C (375°F/Gas 5). Divide the dough in half and roll out one half on a lightly floured work surface to form a 20 cm (8 inch) round. Carefully transfer to one of the prepared trays. Using a sharp knife, score the surface of the dough into eight equal wedges, prick the surface lightly with a fork and, using your fingers, press the edge to form a fluted effect. Repeat using the remaining dough to make a second round. Lightly dust the shortbreads with the extra sugar.

Bake for 18–20 minutes, or until the shortbreads are lightly golden. Remove from the oven and while still hot, follow the score marks and cut into wedges. Cool on the baking trays for 5 minutes, then transfer to a wire rack.

These shortbread will keep, stored in an airtight container, for up to 1 week.

TIP: While shortbread can be made with plain flour alone, adding rice flour produces a lighter result.

Chocolate shortbread

MAKES 65

Preheat the oven to 160°C (315°F/Gas 2–3). Lightly grease two baking trays.

Place the chocolate in a heatproof bowl over a saucepan of simmering water, ensuring the bowl doesn't touch the water. Stir until the chocolate has melted. Set aside to cool for 5 minutes.

Cream the butter and sugar in a medium-sized bowl using electric beaters until pale and fluffy, then add the melted chocolate. Sift in the flour and stir with a wooden spoon to form a soft dough.

Shape tablespoons of the dough into balls, place on the prepared trays well apart and flatten slightly. Bake for 12–15 minutes. Allow to cool on the trays for a few minutes, then transfer to a wire rack to cool completely. Repeat with the remaining dough.

Just before serving, sift the combined cocoa and drinking chocolate over the shortbread to dust.

These shortbread will keep, stored in an airtight container, for up to 1 week.

150 g (5½ oz/1 cup) chopped dark chocolate
250 g (9 oz/1 cup) unsalted butter, softened
115 g (4 oz/½ cup) caster (superfine) sugar
310 g (11 oz/2½ cups) plain (all-purpose) flour
2 tablespoons unsweetened cocoa powder
1 tablespoon drinking chocolate

Custard dream stars

185 g (6½ oz/¾ cup) unsalted butter, softened
40 g (1½ oz/⅓ cup) icing (confectioners') sugar
1 teaspoon natural vanilla extract
125 g (4½ oz/1 cup) plain (all-purpose) flour
40 g (1½ oz/⅓ cup) custard powder
small sugar decorations

Preheat the oven to 180°C (350°F/Gas 4). Line two baking trays with baking paper.

Cream the butter, sugar and vanilla in a medium-sized bowl using electric beaters until pale and fluffy. Sift in the flour and custard powder and stir with a wooden spoon to form a soft dough, being careful not to overmix.

Transfer the mixture to a piping bag fitted with a 1.5 cm (⅝ inch) star nozzle. Pipe the mixture well apart onto the prepared baking trays to form star shapes, about 4 cm (1½ inches) in diameter. Place a sugar decoration in the centre of each star. Refrigerate for 20 minutes.

Bake for 12–15 minutes, or until lightly golden, taking care not to burn. Allow to cool on the trays for a few minutes, then transfer to a wire rack to cool completely.

Custard dream stars will keep, stored in an airtight container, for up to 5 days.

NOTE: You can buy small sugar decorations from most delicatessens and supermarkets.

Cardamom crescents

MAKES 30

60 g (2¼ oz/½ cup) slivered almonds
250 g (9 oz/1 cup) unsalted butter, softened
3 tablespoons icing (confectioners') sugar, sifted
2 tablespoons brandy
1 teaspoon finely grated lime zest
310 g (11 oz/2½ cups) plain (all-purpose) flour
1 teaspoon ground cardamom
icing (confectioners') sugar, extra, to dust and
   to store (optional)

Preheat the oven to 180°C (350°F/Gas 4). Line two baking trays with baking paper. Put the almonds on another baking tray and bake for 5 minutes, or until lightly golden. Allow to cool and finely chop.

Cream the butter and sugar in a medium-sized bowl using electric beaters until pale and fluffy, then mix in the brandy, lime zest and the toasted almonds. Sift in the flour and cardamom and stir with a wooden spoon to form a soft dough.

Shape tablespoons of the dough into small crescents and place on the prepared trays well apart. Bake for 15–20 minutes, or until lightly golden. Allow to cool on the trays for a few minutes, then transfer to a wire rack to cool completely.

To serve, sift over some of the icing sugar to cover the crescents completely. If storing the crescents, place in a tin or plastic box and cover entirely with the remaining icing sugar.

The crescents will keep, stored in an airtight container, for up to 5 days.

Coffee wafers

MAKES 60

185 g (6½ oz/¾ cup) unsalted butter, softened
170 g (6 oz/¾ cup) caster (superfine) sugar
45 g (1¾ oz/¼ cup) dark brown sugar
1 teaspoon natural vanilla extract
1 egg yolk
1 tablespoon milk
60 ml (2 fl oz/¼ cup) strong espresso coffee
375 g (13 oz/3 cups) plain (all-purpose) flour
125 g (4½ oz/1 cup) icing (confectioners')
sugar, sifted
1 tablespoon espresso coffee, extra
coffee beans, to garnish

Preheat the oven to 180°C (350°F/Gas 4). Line two baking trays with baking paper.

Cream the butter and sugars in a large bowl using electric beaters until pale and fluffy, then add the vanilla, egg yolk, milk and coffee, beating until just combined. Sift in the flour and stir with a wooden spoon to form a soft dough.

Turn the dough out onto a lightly floured work surface and knead gently until the mixture comes together. Divide the mixture into two and roll each portion between two pieces of baking paper to 5 mm (¼ inch). Cut the dough into rounds using a 5 cm (2 inch) round cookie cutter, re-rolling the dough scraps and cutting out more rounds. Place on the prepared trays 3 cm (1¼ inches) apart and bake for 10 minutes, or until golden around the edges. Allow to cool on the trays for a few minutes, then transfer to a wire rack to cool completely. Repeat with the remaining dough.

To make the coffee icing, place the icing sugar and coffee in a small bowl and stir until smooth. Using a spoon, spread a circle of icing on top of each wafer and top with coffee beans.

These wafers will keep, stored in an airtight container, for up to 2 weeks.

Honey snaps

MAKES 24

Preheat the oven to 180°C (350°F/Gas 4). Line two baking trays with baking paper.

Cream the butter and sugars in a medium-sized bowl using electric beaters until pale and fluffy, then add the honey, egg yolk and vanilla, beating until just combined. Sift in the flour and bicarbonate of soda and stir with a wooden spoon to form a soft dough.

Shape tablespoons of the dough into logs, place on the prepared trays 5 cm (2 inches) apart and flatten slightly. Bake for 10 minutes, or until lightly golden around the edges. Allow to cool on the trays for a few minutes, then transfer to a wire rack to cool completely.

To make the icing, place the icing sugar in a medium-sized bowl. Add enough lemon juice to make a smooth and spreadable consistency. Once the snaps are completely cooled, spread the tops with the icing.

Honey snaps will keep, stored in an airtight container, for up to 3 weeks.

125 g (4½ oz/½ cup) unsalted butter, softened
55 g (2 oz/¼ cup) caster (superfine) sugar
45 g (1¾ oz/¼ cup) soft brown sugar
115 g (4 oz/⅓ cup) honey
1 egg yolk
1 teaspoon natural vanilla extract
250 g (9 oz/2 cups) plain (all-purpose) flour
½ teaspoon bicarbonate of soda (baking soda)
125 g (4½ oz/1 cup) icing (confectioners') sugar
1–2 tablespoons lemon juice

Chocolate mud cookies

MAKES 36

250 g (9 oz/1⅔ cups) chopped dark chocolate
125 g (4½ oz/½ cup) unsalted butter, softened
185 g (6½ oz/1 cup) soft brown sugar
1 teaspoon natural vanilla extract
1 egg
185 g (6½ oz/1½ cups) plain (all-purpose) flour
40 g (1½ oz/⅓ cup) unsweetened cocoa powder

Preheat the oven to 180°C (350°F/Gas 4). Line two baking trays with baking paper.

Place the chocolate in a food processor and pulse until finely chopped, then set aside.

Cream the butter, sugar and vanilla in a medium-sized bowl using electric beaters until pale and fluffy, then add the egg, beating until just combined. Sift in the flour and cocoa, add the chopped chocolate and stir with a wooden spoon to form a soft dough.

Shape tablespoons of the dough into balls, place on the prepared trays well apart and flatten into 4.5 cm (1¾ inch) rounds. Bake for 9 minutes. Allow to cool on the trays for a few minutes, then transfer to a wire rack to cool completely. Repeat with the remaining dough.

These cookies will keep, stored in an airtight container, for up to 1 week.

Lime and sour cream cookies

MAKES 30

Preheat the oven to 180°C (350°F/Gas 4). Line two baking trays with baking paper.

Cream the butter, sugar and vanilla in a medium-sized bowl using electric beaters until pale and fluffy, then add the lime zest and sour cream, beating until just combined. Sift in the flour and baking powder and stir with a wooden spoon to form a soft dough.

Shape tablespoons of the mixture into balls, place on the prepared trays 5 cm (2 inches) apart and flatten slightly. Bake for 15 minutes, or until lightly golden around the edges. Allow to cool on the trays for a few minutes, then transfer to a wire rack to cool completely. Repeat with the remaining dough.

These cookies will keep, stored in an airtight container, for up to 1 week.

125 g (4½ oz/½ cup) unsalted butter, softened
230 g (8¼ oz/1 cup) caster (superfine) sugar
1 teaspoon natural vanilla extract
1½ tablespoons finely grated lime zest
90 g (3¼ oz/⅓ cup) sour cream
250 g (9 oz/2 cups) plain (all-purpose) flour
½ teaspoon baking powder

Ginger nut cookies

125 g (4½ oz/½ cup) unsalted butter, softened
185 g (6½ oz/1 cup) soft brown sugar
2 tablespoons golden syrup
1 egg yolk
250 g (9 oz/2 cups) plain (all-purpose) flour
½ teaspoon bicarbonate of soda (baking soda)
2 teaspoons ground ginger
1 teaspoon ground mixed spice

Preheat the oven to 170°C (325°F/Gas 3). Line two baking trays with baking paper.

Cream the butter and sugar in a medium-sized bowl using electric beaters until pale and fluffy, then add the golden syrup and egg yolk, beating until just combined. Sift in the flour, bicarbonate of soda, ginger and mixed spice and stir with a wooden spoon until a soft dough forms.

Shape tablespoons of the dough into balls, place on the prepared trays 5 cm (2 inches) apart and flatten into 4 cm (1½ inch) rounds. Bake for 15 minutes, or until lightly golden around the edges. Allow to cool on the trays for a few minutes, then transfer to a wire rack to cool completely.

These cookies will keep, stored in an airtight container, for up to 3 weeks.

Vanilla sugar hearts

MAKES 36

185 g (6½ oz/¾ cup) unsalted butter, softened
230 g (8½ oz/1 cup) caster (superfine) sugar
2 teaspoons natural vanilla extract
1 egg
310 g (11 oz/2½ cups) plain (all-purpose) flour
75 g (2⅔ oz/⅓ cup) white sugar

Cream the butter, sugar and vanilla in a medium-sized bowl using electric beaters until pale and fluffy, then add the egg, beating until just combined. Sift in the flour and stir with a wooden spoon to form a soft dough. Divide the mixture in two, shape the halves into discs, cover with plastic wrap and refrigerate for 1 hour.

Preheat the oven to 180°C (350°F/Gas 4). Line two baking trays with baking paper.

Roll the dough out between two pieces of baking paper to 5 mm (¼ inch) thick. Cut the dough into heart shapes using a 5.5 cm (2¼ inch) heart-shaped cookie cutter, re-rolling the scraps and cutting more hearts. Place on the prepared trays 4 cm (1½ inches) apart, sprinkle with the sugar and gently press it into the dough. Bake for 8–10 minutes, or until lightly golden around the edges. Allow to cool on the trays for a few minutes, then transfer to a wire rack to cool completely. Repeat with the remaining dough.

These cookies will keep, stored in an airtight container, for up to 1 week.

Molasses moons

125 g (4½ oz/½ cup) unsalted butter, softened
185 g (6½ oz/1 cup) soft brown sugar
2 tablespoons molasses
1 egg yolk
250 g (9 oz/2 cups) plain (all-purpose) flour
½ teaspoon bicarbonate of soda (baking soda)
1 teaspoon ground mixed spice

Cream the butter and sugar in a medium-sized bowl using electric beaters until pale and fluffy, then add the molasses and egg yolk, beating until just combined. Sift in the flour, bicarbonate of soda and mixed spice and stir with a wooden spoon to form a soft dough. Cover with plastic wrap and refrigerate for 2 hours.

Preheat the oven to 160°C (315°F/Gas 2–3). Line two baking trays with baking paper.

Divide the dough in two portions and roll each between two pieces of baking paper to 5 mm (¼ inch) thick. Cut the dough into moon shapes using a 6 cm (2½ inch) moon-shaped cutter, re-rolling the scraps and cutting more moons. Place on the prepared trays 5 cm (2 inches) apart and bake for 7 minutes. Allow to cool on the trays for a few minutes, then transfer to a wire rack to cool completely. Repeat with the remaining dough.

Molasses moons will keep, stored in an airtight container, for up to 3 weeks.

Lemon stars

MAKES 22

Preheat the oven to 160°C (315°F/Gas 2–3). Line a baking tray with baking paper.

Cream the butter and sugar in a medium-sized bowl using electric beaters until pale and fluffy, then add the egg yolks and lemon zest, beating until just combined. Sift in the flour, add the cornmeal and stir with a wooden spoon to form a soft dough.

Turn the dough out onto a lightly floured work surface and knead gently until the mixture comes together. Roll out the dough between two pieces of baking paper to 1 cm (½ inch) thick.

Cut the dough into stars using a 3 cm (1¼ inch) star-shaped cutter, re-rolling the dough scraps and cutting more stars. Place on the prepared trays well apart and bake for 15–20 minutes, or until lightly golden around the edges. Allow to cool on the trays for a few minutes, then transfer to a wire rack, dust with icing sugar and leave to cool completely.

Lemon stars will keep, stored in an airtight container, for up to 5 days.

125 g (4½ oz/½ cup) unsalted butter, cubed and softened
115 g (4 oz/½ cup) caster (superfine) sugar
2 egg yolks
2 teaspoons finely grated lemon zest
155 g (5½ oz/1¼ cups) plain (all-purpose) flour
110 g (3¾ oz/¾ cup) coarse cornmeal
icing (confectioners') sugar, to dust

Dipped & drizzled

These indulgent morsels are the perfect offering
for that special occasion ... or just because.

Walnut, chocolate and rosewater meringue

MAKES 48

125 g (4½ oz/½ cup) unsalted butter, softened
60 g (2¼ oz/½ cup) icing (confectioners') sugar
1 teaspoon natural vanilla extract
1 egg yolk
125 g (4½ oz/1 cup) toasted walnuts,
finely chopped
185 g (6½ oz/1½ cups) plain (all-purpose) flour
45 g (1⅔ oz/¼ cup) rice flour
½ teaspoon ground cinnamon
250 g (9 oz/1⅔ cups) chopped dark chocolate

Meringue topping
4 egg whites
2 drops of red food colouring
2 teaspoons rosewater
185 g (6½ oz/1 cup) caster (superfine) sugar

Cream the butter, sugar and vanilla in a medium-sized bowl using electric beaters until pale and fluffy, then add the egg yolk, beating until just combined. Add the walnuts and stir to combine. Sift in the flours and cinnamon and stir with a wooden spoon to form a soft dough. Shape the mixture into a flat disc and refrigerate for 1½ hours.

Preheat the oven to 160°C (315°F/Gas 2–3). Line two baking trays with baking paper.

Roll out the dough between two pieces of baking paper to 5 mm (¼ inch) thick. Cut the dough into circles using a 4 cm (1½ inch) round cookie cutter, re-rolling the dough scraps and cutting more rings. Place on the prepared trays 4 cm (1½ inches) apart and bake for 12 minutes, or until lightly golden around the edges. Allow to cool on the trays for a few minutes, then transfer to a wire rack to cool completely. Repeat with the remaining dough.

Place the chocolate in a heatproof bowl over a saucepan of simmering water, ensuring the bowl doesn't touch the water. Stir until the chocolate has melted. Spread approximately a teaspoon of chocolate on the tops of half of the cookies, and set aside.

Increase the oven to 190°C (375°F/Gas 5). To make the meringue topping, whisk the egg whites, food colouring and rosewater in a bowl until soft peaks form. Gradually add the sugar, one tablespoon at a time, whisking until it is completely dissolved.

Place the cookies back on the baking trays. Using a 1 cm (½ inch) plain nozzle and piping bag, pipe the meringue in a neat circle on top of the cookies, so it comes almost to the edge and sits about 3 cm (1¼ inches) high. Bake for 5 minutes. Cool for a minute on the trays, then transfer the cookies to a wire rack. Repeat with the remaining cookies.

These cookies are best eaten within a couple of hours. Cookies without the meringue topping will keep, stored in an airtight container, for up to 2 weeks.

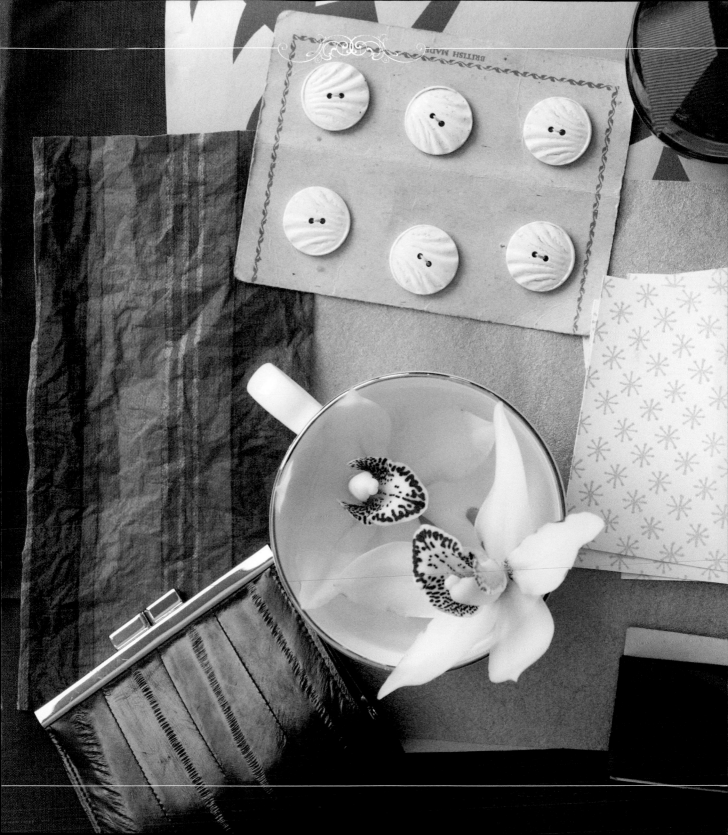

Lime and coconut shortbreads

MAKES 25

250 g (9 oz/2 cups) plain (all-purpose) flour
40 g (1½ oz/⅓ cup) icing (confectioners') sugar
65 g (2¼ oz/¾ cup) desiccated coconut
2 teaspoons finely grated lime zest
200 g (7 oz) unsalted butter, cubed and chilled
1 tablespoon lime juice
125 g (4½ oz/1 cup) icing (confectioners')
    sugar, extra
2 tablespoons lime juice, extra, strained

Preheat the oven to 180°C (350°F/Gas 4). Line two baking trays with baking paper.

Sift the flour and icing sugar into a bowl and stir in the coconut and lime zest. Add the butter and rub in with your fingertips until crumbly. Add the lime juice and cut into the flour mixture using a flat-bladed knife.

Gather the dough into a ball and roll out on a lightly floured work surface to 5 mm (¼ inch) thick. Using a 5 cm (2 inch) biscuit cutter, cut into rounds. Lay well apart on the prepared trays and bake for 15–20 minutes, or until very lightly golden. Allow to cool on the trays for a few minutes, then transfer to a wire rack to cool completely.

To make the icing, sift the extra icing sugar into a small heatproof bowl, add the extra lime juice and place over a saucepan of simmering water. Stir until smooth. Spoon a little icing onto each shortbread, stirring the icing in the bowl occasionally to prevent it from hardening, and spread evenly. Leave the shortbread on the wire rack to set.

These shortbread will keep, stored in an airtight container, for up to 5 days.

Spice biscuits

MAKES 20

125 g (4½ oz/½ cup) unsalted butter, softened
60 g (2¼ oz/⅓ cup) soft brown sugar
1 egg
125 g (4½ oz/1 cup) plain (all-purpose) flour
175 g (6 oz/1 cup) rice flour
1 teaspoon baking powder
1 teaspoon ground cinnamon
1 teaspoon ground mixed spice
1 teaspoon ground ginger
80 g (2¾ oz/¼ cup) raspberry jam

Ginger glacé icing
125 g (4½ oz/1 cup) icing (confectioners') sugar
½ teaspoon ground ginger
20 g (¾ oz) unsalted butter

Line two baking trays with baking paper. Cream the butter and sugar in a medium-sized bowl using electric beaters until pale and fluffy, then add the egg, beating until just combined. Sift in the flours and baking powder, add the spices and stir with a wooden spoon until smooth. Cover with plastic wrap and chill for about 30 minutes.

Preheat the oven to 180°C (350°F/Gas 4). Roll out the dough between two pieces of baking paper to 5 mm (¼ inch) thick. Cut out the dough using a 5 cm (2 inch) fluted round cookie cutter, re-rolling the dough scraps and cutting more rounds. Place on the prepared trays well apart and bake for 12–15 minutes, or until lightly golden. Allow to cool on the trays for a few minutes, then transfer to a wire rack to cool completely.

To make the ginger glacé icing, sift the icing sugar and ginger into a bowl and mix together with the butter and 1 tablespoon boiling water. Sandwich the biscuits with jam and spread on the icing.

These biscuits will keep, stored in an airtight container, for up to 5 days.

Citrus poppy seed cookies

MAKES 36

Cream the butter, sugar and vanilla in a medium-sized bowl using electric beaters until pale and fluffy, then add the orange and lime zest, and orange and lime juice, beating until just combined. Sift in the flour, baking powder and poppy seeds and stir with a wooden spoon to form a soft dough. Divide the mixture into two and wrap each half in plastic wrap. Refrigerate for 1 hour.

Roll out each piece of dough on a lightly floured work surface to form a log. Put on a tray and fold the baking paper over to cover the dough and then cover it in plastic wrap and refrigerate for 2 hours.

Preheat the oven to 170°C (325°F/Gas 3). Line two baking trays with baking paper.

With a sharp knife, trim the ends and then thinly slice the dough into 5 mm (¼ inch) cookies and place on the trays 4 cm (1½ inches) apart. Bake for 10–12 minutes, or until lightly golden around the edges. Allow to cool on the trays for a few minutes, then transfer to a wire rack to cool completely. Repeat with the remaining dough.

These cookies will keep, stored in an airtight container, for up to 2 weeks.

125 g (4½ oz/½ cup) unsalted butter, softened
170 g (6 oz/¾ cup) caster (superfine) sugar
1 teaspoon natural vanilla extract
1 tablespoon finely grated orange zest
1 tablespoon finely grated lime zest
1 tablespoon orange juice
1 tablespoon lime juice
250 g (9 oz/2 cups) plain (all-purpose) flour
¼ teaspoon baking powder
2 tablespoons poppy seeds

Melting moments
with blackberry jam

MAKES 18

250 g (9 oz/1 cup) unsalted butter, softened
60 g (2¼ oz/½ cup) icing (confectioners') sugar
1 teaspoon natural vanilla extract
220 g (7¾ oz/1¾ cups) plain (all-purpose) flour
½ teaspoon baking powder
60 g (2¼ oz/½ cup) cornflour (cornstarch)
30 g (1 oz/¼ cup) icing (confectioners') sugar, extra for dusting
160 g (5⅔ oz/½ cup) blackberry jam

Cream filling
75 g (2⅔ oz) unsalted butter, softened
60 g (2¼ oz/½ cup) icing (confectioners') sugar, sifted
½ teaspoon natural vanilla extract

Cream the butter, icing sugar and vanilla in a medium-sized bowl using electric beaters until pale and fluffy. Sift in the sifted flour, baking powder and cornflour and stir with a wooden spoon until a soft dough forms. Cover with plastic wrap and refrigerate for 1 hour.

To make the cream filling, cream the butter, icing sugar and vanilla until light and fluffy.

Preheat the oven to 160°C (315°F/Gas 2–3). Line two baking trays with baking paper.

Shape 2 teaspoons of dough into balls and place on the prepared trays 4 cm (1½ inches) apart. Flatten the balls slightly with a fork dipped in flour and bake for 10–12 minutes, or until lightly golden. Allow to cool on the trays for a few minutes, then transfer to a wire rack to cool completely. Repeat with the remaining dough.

Dust all the cookies with the extra icing sugar. On half of the cookies, place ½ teaspoon of the cream filling. On the other half, place ½ teaspoon of jam. Press together gently to spread the filling to the edge of the cookie.

Filled cookies will keep, stored in an airtight container, for up to 4 days. Unfilled cookies will keep, stored in an airtight container, for 3 weeks.

Florentines

MAKES 12

55 g (2 oz) unsalted butter
45 g (1¾ oz/¼ cup) soft brown sugar
2 teaspoons honey
25 g (1 oz/¼ cup) flaked almonds, roughly chopped
2 tablespoons chopped dried apricots
2 tablespoons chopped glacé cherries
2 tablespoons mixed peel
40 g (1½ oz/⅓ cup) plain (all-purpose) flour, sifted
120 g (4¼ oz) chopped dark chocolate

Preheat the oven to 180°C (350°F/Gas 4). Grease and line two baking trays with baking paper.

Mix the butter, brown sugar and honey in a saucepan over low heat until the butter is melted and all the ingredients are combined. Remove from the heat and add the almonds, apricots, glacé cherries, mixed peel and the flour. Mix well.

Shape tablespoons of the dough into balls, place on the prepared trays well apart and flatten into 5 cm (2 inch) rounds. Bake for 10 minutes, or until lightly browned. Allow to cool on the trays for a few minutes, then transfer to a wire rack to cool completely.

Place the chocolate in a heatproof bowl over a saucepan of simmering water, ensuring the bowl doesn't touch the water. Stir until the chocolate has melted. Spread the melted chocolate on the bottom of each florentine and, using a fork, make a wavy pattern on the chocolate before it sets. Leave the chocolate to set before serving.

Florentines will keep, stored in an airtight container, for up to 5 days.

Vanilla glazed rings

MAKES 40–44

125 g (4½ oz/½ cup) unsalted butter, softened
115 g (4 oz/½ cup) caster (superfine) sugar
2 teaspoons natural vanilla extract
1 small egg, lightly beaten
210 g (7½ oz/1¾ cups) plain (all-purpose) flour
½ teaspoon baking powder
1 quantity icing glaze (page 134)
yellow food colouring (optional)
1 quantity royal icing (page 134)

Preheat the oven to 180°C (350°F/Gas 4). Lightly grease two baking trays.

Cream the butter, sugar and vanilla in a bowl using electric beaters, then add the egg, beating well. Sift in the flour, baking powder and a pinch of salt and stir with a wooden spoon to form a dough.

Break off small pieces of the dough and roll each piece on a lightly floured work surface to form a 10 cm (4 inch) log. Curl into a ring and gently press the ends together. Transfer to the prepared trays and bake for 10–12 minutes, or until lightly golden. Allow to cool on the trays for a few minutes, then transfer to a wire rack to cool completely.

Make the icing glaze, adding a little yellow food colouring (if using) to the glaze. Make the royal icing and spoon into an icing bag (or see the tip on page 135 to make your own paper icing bag).

Using a paintbrush, brush the tops of the cookies with the glaze and leave to set on a wire rack. Pipe the royal icing backwards and forwards across the cookies to form a zigzag pattern and leave to set.

Vanilla glazed rings will keep, stored in an airtight container, for up to 3 days.

Pecan coffee biscotti

MAKES 40

210 g (7½ oz/1¾ cups) plain (all-purpose) flour
½ teaspoon baking powder
145 g (5¼ oz/⅔ cup) caster (superfine) sugar
60 g (2¼ oz/¼ cup) unsalted butter
2 eggs
½ teaspoon natural vanilla extract
½ teaspoon instant coffee granules
135 g (4¾ oz/1⅓ cups) whole pecans
½ teaspoon caster (superfine) sugar, extra

Preheat the oven to 180°C (350°F/Gas 4). Line two baking trays with baking paper.

Place the sifted flour, baking powder, sugar and a pinch of salt in a food processor and process for 1–2 seconds. Add the butter and mix until the mixture resembles fine breadcrumbs. Add the eggs and vanilla and process until the mixture is smooth.

Transfer the dough to a well-floured surface and knead in the coffee and pecans. Divide into two equal portions and, using lightly floured hands, shape each into a log about 20 cm (8 inches) long. Place the logs on the baking trays and sprinkle with the extra sugar. Press the top of each log down gently to make an oval. Bake for about 35 minutes, or until golden. Remove and set aside to cool for about 20 minutes. Reduce the oven temperature to 170°C (325°F/Gas 3).

Cut the logs into 1 cm (½ inch) slices. Turn the baking paper over and spread the biscotti well apart on the tray so they don't touch. Return to the oven and bake for a further 30 minutes, or until they just begin to colour. Allow to cool on the trays for a few minutes, then transfer to a wire rack to cool completely.

These biscotti will keep, stored in an airtight container, for up to 3 weeks.

Tiramisu creams

125 g (4½ oz/½ cup) unsalted butter, softened
60 g (2¼ oz/½ cup) icing (confectioners') sugar
1 teaspoon natural vanilla extract
90 g (3¼ oz/¾ cup) plain (all-purpose) flour
45 g (1⅔ oz/¼ cup) rice flour
30 g (1 oz/¼ cup) unsweetened cocoa powder
55 g (2 oz/½ cup) ground almonds
2 tablespoons unsweetened cocoa powder, extra, for dusting

Mascarpone cream
1 tablespoon instant coffee granules
110 g (3¾ oz/½ cup) mascarpone cheese
3 teaspoons icing (confectioners') sugar

Chocolate spread
100 g (3½ oz/⅔ cup) chopped dark chocolate
20 g (¾ oz) unsalted butter, softened
1 tablespoon coffee liqueur

Preheat the oven to 170°C (325°F/Gas 3). Line two baking trays with baking paper.

Cream the butter, sugar and vanilla in a medium-sized bowl using electric beaters. Sift in the flours, cocoa and almonds and stir with a wooden spoon to form a soft dough.

Shape teaspoons of the dough into balls, place on the prepared trays 4 cm (1½ inches) apart and flatten slightly. Bake for 10 minutes. Allow to cool on the trays for a few minutes, then transfer to a wire rack to cool completely. Repeat with the remaining dough.

To make the mascarpone cream, combine the instant coffee with 1 teaspoon boiling water, stir to dissolve and allow to cool. Add the mascarpone and sugar.

To make the chocolate spread, place the chocolate in a heatproof bowl over a saucepan of simmering water, ensuring the bowl doesn't touch the water. Stir until the chocolate has melted. Remove from the heat and place in a clean bowl. Allow to cool for a couple of minutes and then add the butter and liqueur, stir and use immediately.

Spread 1½ teaspoons of the chocolate spread onto half the cookies. Top with 2 teaspoons of mascarpone cream and sandwich with the remaining cookies. Dust with cocoa.

Serve filled cookies immediately. Unfilled cookies will keep, stored in an airtight container, for up to 2 weeks.

Blueberry and almond cookies

MAKES 24

90 g (3¼ oz/⅓ cup) unsalted butter, softened
170 g (6 oz/¾ cup) caster (superfine) sugar
½ teaspoon almond extract
1 teaspoon natural vanilla extract
1 tablespoon milk
125 g (4½ oz/1 cup) plain (all-purpose) flour
½ teaspoon baking powder
80 g (2¾ oz/¾ cup) ground almonds
50 g (1¾ oz/⅓ cup) dried blueberries
melted white chocolate, for dipping (optional)

Preheat the oven to 180°C (350°F/Gas 4). Line two trays with baking paper.

Cream the butter, sugar, almond and vanilla extracts in a medium-sized bowl using electric beaters until pale and fluffy, then add the milk, beating until just combined. Sift in the flour and baking powder, add the ground almonds and blueberries, and stir with a wooden spoon to form a soft dough.

Shape 2 teaspoons of dough into balls, place on the prepared trays 4 cm (1½ inches) apart and flatten slightly. Bake for 10–12 minutes, or until lightly golden around the edges. Allow to cool on the trays for a few minutes, then transfer to a wire rack to cool completely.

These cookies will keep, stored in an airtight container, for up to 2 weeks.

Ginger kisses

MAKES 20

125 g (4½ oz/½ cup) unsalted butter, softened
115 g (4 oz/½ cup) caster (superfine) sugar
1 teaspoon natural vanilla extract
1 egg
85 g (3 oz/⅔ cup) plain (all-purpose) flour
90 g (3¼ oz/¾ cup) cornflour (cornstarch)
¼ teaspoon baking powder
1½ teaspoons ground ginger
1 teaspoon ground mixed spice
½ teaspoon ground ginger, extra, for dusting
2 teaspoons icing (confectioners') sugar,
for dusting

Honey cream
90 g (3¼ oz/⅓ cup) unsalted butter, softened
1½ tablespoons icing (confectioners') sugar
1½ tablespoons honey

Preheat the oven to 200°C (400°F/Gas 6). Line two baking trays with baking paper.

Cream the butter, sugar and vanilla in a medium-sized bowl using electric beaters until pale and fluffy, then add the egg, beating until just combined. Sift in the flours and baking powder, add the ginger and mixed spice and stir with a wooden spoon to form a soft dough.

Shape teaspoons of the dough into balls, place on the prepared trays 4 cm (1½ inches) apart and flatten slightly. Bake for 7 minutes, or until lightly golden around the edges. Allow to cool on the trays for a few minutes, then transfer to a wire rack to cool completely. Repeat with the remaining dough.

For the honey cream, beat the butter and icing sugar in a bowl using electric beaters until light and fluffy. Add the honey and mix to combine. On half of the cookies, spread 3 teaspoons of honey cream and sandwich them together with the other half.

In a small bowl combine the extra ginger and icing sugar and dust over the cookies.

Filled cookies will keep, stored in an airtight container, for 3 days. Unfilled cookies will keep for up to 5 days.

Amore

MAKES 20

Preheat the oven to 170°C (325°F/Gas 3). Line two baking trays with baking paper.

Sift the flour, ¼ teaspoon salt, baking powder and mixed spice into a bowl. Add the sugar, lemon zest, egg, milk, vanilla and butter and, using electric beaters, mix into a smooth dough. Turn out onto a lightly floured surface and roll into a smooth ball. Cover with plastic wrap and refrigerate for 20 minutes.

Divide the dough in half. On a lightly floured surface, roll out one portion to 3 mm (⅛ inch) thick. Cut the dough into ten hearts using a 7 cm (2¾ inch) heart-shaped cookie cutter. Re-roll out the scraps and cut out ten 1 cm (½ inch) hearts. Place on the prepared trays. Working with the other portion, knead in the cocoa and brandy until just combined, then repeat as above.

Lay a small heart onto a large heart of the opposite colour. Bake for 12 minutes, or until lightly golden. Allow to cool on the trays for a few minutes, then transfer to a wire rack to cool completely. Sift over the icing sugar.

These will keep, stored in an airtight container, for up to 5 days.

250 g (9 oz/2 cups) plain (all-purpose) flour
1 teaspoon baking powder
¼ teaspoon ground mixed spice
60 g (2¼ oz/⅓ cup) soft brown sugar
½ teaspoon finely grated lemon zest
1 egg
1 tablespoon milk
1 teaspoon natural vanilla extract
100 g (3½ oz) unsalted butter, softened
2 teaspoons unsweetened cocoa powder
1 teaspoon brandy
icing (confectioners') sugar, to dust

Lemon curd sandwiches

MAKES 24

Lemon curd
juice from 2 lemons
80 g (2¾ oz/⅓ cup) caster (superfine) sugar
3 teaspoons cornflour (cornstarch)
4 egg yolks
finely grated zest from 1 lemon

110 g (3¾ oz) unsalted butter, softened
115 g (4 oz/½ cup) caster (superfine) sugar
½ teaspoon natural vanilla extract
2 teaspoons finely grated lemon zest
1 egg yolk
155 g (5½ oz/1¼ cups) plain (all-purpose) flour
30 g (1 oz/¼ cup) icing (confectioners') sugar, for dusting

To make the lemon curd, combine the lemon juice, sugar and the cornflour in a small saucepan and, over low heat, whisk until combined. Slowly bring to the boil, stirring with a wooden spoon until the mixture thickens. Remove from the heat and whisk in the egg yolks and zest. Return to a gentle heat and cook for 2–3 minutes, stirring until well combined and thickened. Remove from the heat and place the curd in a heatproof bowl. Place plastic wrap on the surface of the curd to stop a skin forming and set aside to cool. This can be made in advance, and needs to be refrigerated.

Preheat the oven to 170°C (325°F/Gas 3). Line two baking trays with baking paper.

Cream the butter, sugar and vanilla in a bowl using electric beaters until pale and fluffy, then add the lemon zest and egg yolk, beating until just combined. Sift in the flour and, using a wooden spoon, stir until it forms a soft dough. Turn out the dough, and gently shape it into a flat disc. Cover with plastic wrap and refrigerate for 20 minutes.

Roll the dough out between two pieces of baking paper to 3 mm (⅛ inch) thick. Cut the dough into round and ring shapes, alternating between 4.5 cm (1¾ inch) round-shaped cutter and a 4.5 cm (1¾ inch) ring-shaped cutter so you end up with the same amount of each shape. Re-roll any leftover dough scraps and cut more rounds and rings.

Place on the prepared trays 3 cm (1¼ inches) apart and bake for 9 minutes, or until lightly golden around the edges. Allow to cool on the trays for a few minutes, then transfer to a wire rack to cool completely. Repeat with the remaining dough.

On the cookie rounds, place a teaspoon of the lemon curd, flatten a little with a knife and then sandwich it together with a ring cookie, pressing down on the curd so it goes right to the edge. Dust the cookies with the icing sugar. Repeat with the remaining cookies.

Filled cookies will keep, stored in an airtight container for 3 days. Unfilled cookies will keep, stored in an airtight container, for up to 3 weeks.

Gingerbread

MAKES 40 (depending on size of cutters)

350 g (12 oz) plain (all-purpose) flour
2 teaspoons baking powder
2 teaspoons ground ginger
100 g (3½ oz) unsalted butter, chilled and diced
140 g (5 oz/¾ cup) soft brown sugar
1 egg, beaten
115 g (4 oz/⅓ cup) dark treacle
silver balls (optional)

Icing glaze
1 egg white
3 teaspoons lemon juice
155 g (5½ oz/1¼ cups) icing (confectioners') sugar

Royal icing
1 egg white
200 g (7 oz) icing (confectioners') sugar

Preheat the oven to 190°C (375°F/Gas 5). Lightly grease two baking trays.

Sift the flour, baking powder, ground ginger and a pinch of salt into a bowl. Rub in the butter with your fingertips until the mixture resembles fine breadcrumbs, then stir in the sugar. Make a well in the centre, add the egg and treacle and, using a wooden spoon, stir until a soft dough forms. Transfer to a clean surface and knead until smooth.

Divide the dough in half and roll out on a lightly floured work surface until 5 mm (¼ inch) thick. Using various-shaped cookie cutters (hearts, stars or flowers), cut the dough and then transfer to the prepared trays. Bake in batches for 8 minutes, or until the gingerbread is light brown. Allow to cool on the trays for a few minutes, then transfer to a wire rack to cool completely. (If using the gingerbread as hanging decorations, use a skewer to make a small hole in each one while still hot.)

To make the icing glaze, whisk the egg white and lemon juice together until foamy, then whisk in the icing sugar to form a smooth, thin icing. Cover the surface with plastic wrap until needed.

To make the royal icing, lightly whisk the egg white until just foamy, then gradually whisk in enough icing sugar to form a soft icing. Cover the surface with plastic wrap until needed.

Brush a thin layer of glaze over some of the gingerbread and leave to set. Using an icing bag (or see the tip below) filled with royal icing, decorate the gingerbread as shown in the photograph, or as desired.

Gingerbread will keep, stored in an airtight container, for up to 3 days.

TIP: To make a paper icing bag, cut a piece of baking paper into a 19 cm (7½ inch) square and then cut in half diagonally to form two triangles. Hold the triangle, with the longest side away from you, and curl the left hand point over and in towards the centre.

Repeat with the right hand point, forming a cone shape, with both ends meeting neatly in the middle. Staple together at the wide end.

Strawberry pecan dipped in pink chocolate cookies

MAKES 32

160 g (5⅔ oz/⅔ cup) unsalted butter, softened
170 g (6 oz/¾ cup) caster (superfine) sugar
½ teaspoon natural vanilla extract
80 g (2¾ oz/⅓ cup) fresh strawberry purée
100 g (3½ oz/½ cup) dried strawberries,
    thinly sliced
80 g (2¾ oz) ground pecans
185 g (6½ oz/1½ cups) plain (all-purpose) flour
300 g (10½ oz) white chocolate, chopped
red food colouring

Preheat the oven to 180°C (350°F/Gas 4). Line two baking trays with baking paper.

Cream the butter, sugar and vanilla in a bowl using electric beaters until pale and fluffy. Mix in the strawberry purée, dried strawberries and ground pecans. Sift in the flour and stir until it forms a soft dough.

Shape tablespoons of the dough into balls and put on the prepared trays 5 cm (2 inches) apart. Flatten slightly and bake for 12–15 minutes, or until lightly golden around the edges. Allow to cool on the trays for a few minutes, then transfer to a wire rack to cool completely. Repeat with the remaining dough.

Place the chocolate in a heatproof bowl over a saucepan of simmering water, ensuring the bowl doesn't touch the water. Stir until the chocolate has melted. Remove from the heat and stir in the food colouring, a drop at a time, until the chocolate is pale pink. Dip each cookie into the chocolate to coat half of it. Place on a lined baking tray for about 40 minutes to set.

These cookies will keep, stored in an airtight container, for up to 1 week.

Chocolate Pfeffernusse

200 g (7 fl oz) honey
100 g (3½ oz) treacle
125 g (4½ oz/⅔ cup) soft brown sugar
150 g (5½ oz) unsalted butter
500 g (1 lb 2 oz/4 cups) plain (all-purpose) flour
60 g (2¼ oz/½ cup) unsweetened cocoa powder
1 teaspoon baking powder
½ teaspoon bicarbonate of soda (baking soda)
1 teaspoon ground white pepper
1 teaspoon ground cinnamon
½ teaspoon ground nutmeg
100 g (3½ oz/⅔ cup) blanched almonds, chopped
1 teaspoon finely grated lemon zest
45 g (1½ oz/¼ cup) mixed peel
2 eggs, lightly beaten
300 g (10½ oz) dark chocolate, chopped

Line two baking trays with baking paper. Combine the honey, treacle, brown sugar and butter in a small saucepan. Place over medium heat and bring to the boil, stirring occasionally. Remove from the heat and set aside to cool a little.

Sift the flour, cocoa, baking powder, bicarbonate of soda, spices and ¼ teaspoon salt into a large bowl. Stir in the almonds, lemon zest and mixed peel and mix thoroughly. Make a well in the centre and pour in the honey mixture and the eggs. Mix until well combined. Cover the mixture and refrigerate for 2 hours.

Preheat the oven to 180°C (350°F/Gas 4). Shape tablespoons of the dough into balls, place on the prepared trays well apart and bake for 12–15 minutes. Allow to cool on the trays for a few minutes, then transfer to a wire rack to cool completely.

Place the chocolate in a heatproof bowl over a saucepan of simmering water, ensuring the bowl doesn't touch the water. Stir until the chocolate has melted. Dip the tops of the cookies in the chocolate, allow any excess to drain off, then place on baking paper to set.

These will keep, stored in an airtight container, for up to 5 days.

Mandarin whirls

MAKES 18 'SANDWICHES'

Preheat the oven to 180°C (350°F/Gas 4). Line two baking trays with baking paper.

Cream the butter, sugar and zest in a bowl using electric beaters until pale and fluffy. Sift in the flours, then stir with a wooden spoon to form a soft dough.

Transfer the mixture to a piping bag fitted with a 4 cm (1½ inch) star nozzle and pipe thirty-six 4 cm (1½ inch) rounds, spacing them well apart, on the prepared trays. Bake for 12–15 minutes, or until lightly golden around the edges. Allow to cool on the trays for a few minutes, then transfer to a wire rack to cool completely.

To make the icing, cream the butter, sugar and mandarin juice in a bowl using electric beaters until pale and soft. Use the icing to sandwich the whirls together.

Filled cookies are best served on the day they are made. Unfilled cookies will keep, stored in an airtight container, for up to 1 week.

350 g (12 oz) unsalted butter, softened
60 g (2¼ oz/½ cup) icing (confectioners') sugar
finely grated zest from 2 mandarins
250 g (9 oz/2 cups) plain (all-purpose) flour
60 g (2¼ oz/½ cup) cornflour (cornstarch)
120 g (4¼ oz) unsalted butter, softened, extra
250 g (9 oz/2 cups) icing (confectioners') sugar, extra
2 tablespoons freshly squeezed mandarin juice

Coconut passionfruit macaroons

MAKES 20

3 egg whites
285 g (10¼ oz/1¼ cups) caster (superfine) sugar
½ teaspoon natural vanilla extract
180 g (6 oz/2 cups) desiccated coconut
2 tablespoons plain (all-purpose) flour
shredded coconut, to dust

Cream filling
200 ml (7 fl oz) whipping cream
60 g (2¼ oz/¼ cup) passionfruit pulp
2 teaspoons icing (confectioners') sugar
½ teaspoon natural vanilla extract

Preheat the oven to 160°C (315°F/Gas 2–3). Line two baking trays with baking paper.

Whisk the egg whites in a bowl until frothy. While beating, add the sugar and vanilla, and continue beating until soft peaks form. Add the desiccated coconut and flour and, using a wooden spoon, gently stir into the egg mixture until combined.

Shape 2 teaspoons of the mixture into balls, place on the prepared trays 4 cm (1½ inches) apart and flatten slightly. Bake for 12 minutes, or until lightly golden around the edges. Allow to cool on the trays for a few minutes, then transfer to a wire rack to cool completely. Repeat with the remaining mixture.

To make the cream filling, whip the cream until firm peaks form. Add the remaining ingredients and stir to combine.

To assemble, place 3 teaspoons of the cream filling onto the bottoms of half the macaroons. Top with the remaining macaroons and dust with shredded coconut.

These filled macaroons are best eaten immediately. Unfilled macaroons will keep, stored in an airtight container, for up to 3 days.

Shrewsbury shortbread

MAKES 18

125 g (4½ oz/½ cup) unsalted butter, softened
115 g (4 oz/½ cup) caster (superfine) sugar
2 teaspoons finely grated lemon zest
1 egg
250 g (9 oz/2 cups) plain (all-purpose) flour
1 teaspoon baking powder
raspberry jam
icing (confectioners') sugar, to dust

Line two baking trays with baking paper. Cream the butter, sugar and lemon zest in a medium-sized bowl using electric beaters until pale and fluffy, then add the egg, beating until just combined. Sift in the flour and baking powder and stir with a wooden spoon until smooth. Cover and refrigerate for 30 minutes.

Preheat the oven to 180°C (350°F/Gas 4). Place half of the dough between two sheets of baking paper and roll out to a 5 mm (¼ inch) thickness. Using a 5.5 cm (2¼ inch) round fluted cutter, cut out 18 circles.

Roll out the other piece of dough and cut out 18 circles as before. Using a 2 cm (¾ inch) round fluted cutter, cut out the centre of these circles. Bake all the shortbread for 8–10 minutes, or until golden. Allow to cool on the trays for a few minutes, then transfer to a wire rack to cool completely.

Spread the whole circles with 1 teaspoon of jam and top with the cut-out circles, pressing gently to seal. Sift the icing sugar over the shortbread.

These shortbread will keep, stored in an airtight container, for up to 5 days.

Chocolate coated quince cookies

MAKES 24

125 g (4½ oz/½ cup) unsalted butter, softened
40 g (1½ oz/⅓ cup) icing (confectioners') sugar
½ teaspoon natural vanilla extract
125 g (4½ oz/1 cup) plain (all-purpose) flour
35 g (1¼ oz/⅓ cup) ground almonds
145 g (5½ oz/½ cup) quince paste
250 g (9 oz/1⅔ cups) chopped dark chocolate

Preheat the oven to 160°C (315°F/Gas 2–3). Line two baking trays with baking paper.

Cream the butter, icing sugar and vanilla in a bowl using electric beaters until pale and fluffy. Sift in the flour and ground almonds, and stir until it forms a soft dough. Turn out the dough and shape into a flat disc. Cover with plastic wrap and refrigerate for 20 minutes.

Roll the dough between two pieces of baking paper to 5 mm (¼ inch) thick. Cut the dough into round shapes using a 4 cm (1½ inch) round cookie cutter. Place on the prepared trays well apart and bake for 7–10 minutes, or until lightly golden. Allow to cool on the trays for a few minutes, then transfer to a wire rack to cool completely.

Gently heat the quince paste in a small saucepan until it becomes a spreadable consistency. Spread 1 teaspoon of the paste on the bottom of half the cookies and sandwich together with the remaining half. Place the chocolate in a heatproof bowl over a saucepan of simmering water, ensuring the bowl doesn't touch the water. Stir until the chocolate has melted. Set aside to cool for 3 minutes. Re-line the two baking trays. Gently coat the cookies in the chocolate and place them on the trays to set.

These cookies will keep, stored in an airtight container, for up to 10 days.

Lime and
vanilla leaves

MAKES 48

Cream the butter, sugar and vanilla in a bowl using electric beaters until pale and fluffy, then stir in the lime juice and zest. Sift in the flours and stir with a wooden spoon to form a soft dough. Turn onto a lightly floured surface and shape into a disc. Cover with plastic wrap and refrigerate for 30 minutes.

Preheat the oven to 160°C (315°F/Gas 2–3). Line two baking trays with baking paper.

Roll the dough out between two pieces of baking paper to 5 mm (¼ inch) thick. Cut the dough into leaf shapes with a 5.5 cm (2¼ inch) leaf-shaped cookie cutter, re-rolling out any dough scraps and cutting more leaves. Place on the prepared trays 4 cm (1½ inches) apart and bake for 10 minutes, or until lightly golden around the edges. Allow to cool on the trays for a few minutes, then transfer to a wire rack to cool completely. Repeat with the remaining dough.

To make the vanilla glaze, combine the egg white and lime juice in a bowl using electric beaters until frothy. Stir in the icing sugar and beat until thickened. Add the scraped vanilla bean, vanilla seeds and vanilla extract and beat until combined. Dip each leaf into the glaze to coat the top. Leave on a wire rack to set for 40 minutes.

These cookies will keep, stored in an airtight container, for 1 week.

125 g (4½ oz/½ cup) unsalted butter, softened
40 g (1½ oz/⅓ cup) icing (confectioners') sugar
2 teaspoons natural vanilla extract
2 teaspoons lime juice
2 teaspoons finely grated lime zest
185 g (6½ oz/1½ cups) plain (all-purpose) flour
45 g (1⅔ oz/¼ cup) rice flour

Vanilla glaze
1 egg white
1 tablespoon lime juice
165 g (5¾ oz/1⅓ cup) icing (confectioners') sugar
1 vanilla bean
1 teaspoon natural vanilla extract

149

Hazelnut jaffa fingers and chocolate dipping pot

MAKES 30

90 g (3¼ oz/⅓ cup) unsalted butter, softened
115 g (4 oz/½ cup) caster (superfine) sugar
2 teaspoons finely grated orange zest
2 teaspoons orange juice
55 g (2 oz/½ cup) ground hazelnuts
90 g (3¼ oz/¾ cup) plain (all-purpose) flour

Chocolate pot
200 g (7 oz/1⅓ cups) chopped dark chocolate
2 tablespoons pouring cream
2 teaspoons orange liqueur

Preheat the oven to 180°C (350°F/Gas 4). Line two baking trays with baking paper.

Cream the butter and sugar in a bowl using electric beaters until pale and fluffy, then add the orange zest and juice and the hazelnuts, and stir to combine. Sift in the flour and stir with a wooden spoon to form a soft dough.

Shape 2 teaspoons of dough into thin logs, approximately 8 cm (3¼ inches) long, and place on the prepared trays 4 cm (1½ inches) apart. Bake for 10 minutes, or until lightly golden around the edges. Allow to cool on the trays for a few minutes, then transfer to a wire rack to cool completely. Repeat with the remaining dough.

To make the chocolate pot, combine the chocolate, cream and liqueur in a heatproof bowl over a saucepan of simmering water, ensuring the bowl doesn't touch the water. Stir until the chocolate has melted and is smooth. Serve as a warm dip with the cookies.

These cookies will keep, stored in an airtight container, for up to 2 weeks.

Strawberry pillows

MAKES 18

Line two baking trays with baking paper. Place the flour and butter in a food processor and pulse until it resembles coarse breadcrumbs. Add the sour cream and lemon zest and pulse until a dough forms, being careful not to overprocess. Turn out onto a lightly floured work surface, and press into a flat, round disc. Cover with plastic wrap and refrigerate for 30 minutes.

Preheat the oven to 200°C (400°F/Gas 6). Roll out the dough on a lightly floured work surface to 3 mm (¹⁄₈ inch) thick and, using a ruler, cut the dough into 6 cm (2½ inch) squares. Reshape any leftover dough, roll out and cut it into more squares. Place ¾ teaspoon of conserve into the middle of each pastry square. Using the tip of your finger, wet the edges with a little water and fold the pastry in half, pressing to seal with a fork. Brush each pillow with a little of the beaten egg. Place on the prepared trays and bake for 13 minutes, or until lightly golden. Allow to cool on the trays for a few minutes, then transfer to a wire rack to cool completely. Once cool, lightly dust with icing sugar.

The strawberry pillows will keep, stored in an airtight container, for up to 5 days.

155 g (5½ oz/1¼ cups) plain (all-purpose) flour
90 g (3¼ oz/⅓ cup) unsalted butter, chilled and cubed
90 g (3¼ oz/⅓ cup) sour cream
2 teaspoons finely grated lemon zest
80 g (2¾ oz/¼ cup) strawberry conserve
1 egg, lightly beaten
1 tablespoon icing (confectioners') sugar, to dust

Chocolate fudge sandwiches

250 g (9 oz/2 cups) plain (all-purpose) flour
30 g (1 oz/¼ cup) unsweetened cocoa powder
200 g (7 oz) unsalted butter, chilled and cubed
100 g (3½ oz) icing (confectioners') sugar
2 egg yolks, lightly beaten
1 teaspoon natural vanilla extract

Filling
100 g (3½ oz/⅔ cup) chopped dark chocolate
1 tablespoon golden syrup or dark corn syrup
25 g (1 oz) unsalted butter, softened

Preheat the oven to 200°C (400°F/Gas 6). Lightly grease two baking trays. Sift the flour and cocoa powder into a bowl and rub in the butter until the mixture resembles fine breadcrumbs. Sift in the sugar and stir to combine. Using a wooden spoon, gradually stir in the egg yolks and vanilla until a soft dough forms.

Transfer the dough to a lightly floured work surface and shape into a 4 x 6 x 26 cm (1½ x 2½ x 10½ inch) block. Wrap in plastic wrap and refrigerate for 30 minutes. Cut the dough into 40–48 slices, about 5 mm (¼ inch) wide. Place the slices, well apart, on the prepared trays. Bake for 10 minutes, or until firm. Allow to cool on the trays for a few minutes, then transfer to a wire rack to cool completely.

To make the filling, place the chocolate in a heatproof bowl over a saucepan of simmering water, ensuring the bowl doesn't touch the water. Stir until the chocolate has melted. Remove from the heat, stir in the golden syrup and butter and continue stirring until the mixture is smooth. Allow to cool a little, then refrigerate for 10 minutes, or until the mixture is thick enough to spread. Use the chocolate filling to sandwich the cookies together.

Filled cookies are best eaten on the day they are made. Unfilled cookies will keep, stored in an airtight container, for up to 3 days.

Index

Published in 2008 by Murdoch Books Pty Limited

Murdoch Books Australia
Pier 8/9
23 Hickson Road
Millers Point NSW 2000
Phone: +61 (0) 2 8220 2000
Fax: +61 (0) 2 8220 2558
www.murdochbooks.com.au

Murdoch Books UK Limited
Erico House, 6th Floor
93–99 Upper Richmond Road
Putney, London SW15 2TG
Phone: +44 (0) 20 8785 5995
Fax: +44 (0) 20 8785 5985
www.murdochbooks.co.uk

Chief Executive: Juliet Rogers
Publishing Director: Kay Scarlett

Commissioning editor: Jane Lawson
Editor: Lucy Broadhurst
Food editor: Chrissy Freer
Design Concept: Reuben Crossman
Design layout: Melanie Ngapo
Photographer: Brett Stevens
Stylist: Lynsey Fryers
Food preparation: Peta Dent
Recipes by: Lee Currie and the Murdoch Books Test Kitchen
Production: Nikla Martin

Text, design and photography copyright © 2008
Murdoch Books

National Library of Australia Cataloguing-in-Publication Data

Title: Indulgence cookies / editor, Lucy Broadhurst.
ISBN: 978 1 7419 6117 1 (hbk.)
Series: Indulgence series
Notes: Includes index.
Subjects: Cookies.
Other Authors/Contributors:
Broadhurst, Lucy
Dewey Number: 641.8654

A catalogue record for this book is available from the British Library.
Colour separation by COLOUR CHIEFS PTY LTD
Printed by 1010 Printing International Limited in 2008.
PRINTED IN CHINA.

The Publisher and stylist would like to thank Anibou, Australian Salvage Company, Crowley & Grouch, Domayne Design, Empire Homewares, Koskela, Miljo, Mokum Textiles and Tres Fabu! for lending equipment for use and photography.

IMPORTANT: Those who might be at risk from the effects of salmonella poisoning (the elderly, pregnant women, young children and those suffering from immune deficiency diseases) should consult their doctor with any concerns about eating raw eggs.

OVEN GUIDE: You may find cooking times vary depending on the oven you are using. For fan-forced ovens, as a general rule, set the oven temperature to 20°C (35°F) lower than indicated in the recipe.